# Pages For Seniors

A RIDICULOUSLY SIMPLE GUIDE TO WORD
PROCESSING ON YOUR MAC

Scott La Counte

ANAHEIM, CALIFORNIA

www.RidiculouslySimpleBooks.com

Copyright © 2020 by Scott La Counte.

**All rights reserved**. No part of this publication may be reproduced, distributed or transmitted in any form or by any means, including photocopying, recording, or other electronic or mechanical methods, without the prior written permission of the publisher, except in the case of brief quotations embodied in critical reviews and certain other noncommercial uses permitted by copyright law.

**Limited Liability / Disclaimer of Warranty**. While best efforts have been used in preparing this book, the author and publishers make no representations or warranties of any kind and assume no liabilities of any kind with respect to accuracy or completeness of the content and specifically the author nor publisher shall be held liable or responsible to any person or entity with respect to any loss or incidental r consequential damages caused or alleged to have been caused, directly, or indirectly without limitations, by the information or programs contained herein. Furthermore, readers should be aware that the Internet sites listed in this work may have changed or disappeared. This work is sold with the understanding that the advice inside may not be suitable in every situation.

**Trademarks**. Where trademarks are used in this book this infers no endorsement or any affiliation with this book. Any trademarks (including, but not limiting to, screenshots) used in this book are solely used for editorial and educational purposes.

# Table of Contents

**Introduction** ............................................................. 8

**Understanding Word Processing On Your Mac** ...... 9

    **How To Get Pages** ............................................................. 9

    **Running Pages for the First Time** ............................... 11

    **The Pages Crash Course** ............................................. 12

        Select ............................................................................. 15
        Select Paragraph ....................................................... 15
        Select All ...................................................................... 15
        Select Options ............................................................ 16
        Cut, Copy and Paste ................................................ 16
        Find and Replace ...................................................... 16
        Define ........................................................................... 18
        Copy Style .................................................................. 19
        Inserting Hyperlinks ................................................. 20
        Undo/Redo ................................................................. 21
        Hands-On Exercise ................................................... 22

    **The Formatting Toolbar** ............................................... 23

        Hands-On Exercise ................................................... 26

    **Layout** ............................................................................... 26

    **More** .................................................................................. 27

    **Opening Pages From iCloud** ..................................... 28

    **Managing Documents** ................................................ 29

        Renaming Documents ............................................ 30

    **Hands-On Exercise** ....................................................... 31

**Adding / Editing Photos In Pages** ........................... 33

**Inserting An Image** .................................................................. 34

**Arranging Images** ................................................................... 36
    Resize and Rotate ................................................................ 36
    Text Wrap and Placement ................................................... 38
    Image Grouping ................................................................... 43
    Watermarks ........................................................................... 44

**Edit Mask and Alpha** ............................................................. 45

**Styling Your Image** ................................................................ 49
    Basic Styles ........................................................................... 50
    Border .................................................................................... 51
    Shadow .................................................................................. 52
    Reflection ............................................................................. 54
    Transparency ....................................................................... 55

**Hands-on Exercise** ................................................................. 56

*Inserting and Formatting Tables* ............................................ 58

**Inserting a Table** ..................................................................... 59
    Adding Columns and Rows ................................................ 59

**Interacting with Tables** ......................................................... 60

**Row / Column Options** ......................................................... 61

**Styling Tables** .......................................................................... 62
    Table Options ...................................................................... 62
    Cell Options .......................................................................... 63
    Text Options ........................................................................ 66
    Arrange Options .................................................................. 68

**Deleting Tables** ....................................................................... 68

**Importing Tables** .................................................................... 69

**Hands-on Exercise** ................................................................. 69

*Inserting / Formatting Charts* ................................................ 71

**Inserting a Chart** .................................................................... 72

| Editing Chart Data | 74 |
| --- | --- |
| Styling Your Pie Chart | 75 |
| Styling Your Bar Chart | 82 |
| Hands-On Exercise | 83 |

## *Creating Shapes* .......................................................... *85*

| Inserting a Shape | 86 |
| --- | --- |
| Resizing Shapes and Adjusting Proportions | 87 |
| Moving and Rotating Shapes | 89 |
| Adding Text to a Shape | 89 |
| Creating Text Boxes | 89 |
| Styling Shapes and Text Boxes | 92 |
| Hands-On Exercise | 92 |

## *Setting Up a Document* ............................................ *94*

| Entering Document Setup Mode | 95 |
| --- | --- |
| Changing Document Margins and Size | 96 |
| Creating Custom Paper Size | 97 |
| Hyphenations and Ligatures | 99 |
| Headers and Page Numbers | 99 |
| Bookmarks | 101 |
| Table of Contents | 102 |
| Insert Footnotes | 105 |
| Insert Comment | 106 |
| Track Changes | 106 |

## *Understanding Templates* ..................................... *108*

| Using Third-Party Pages Templates | 109 |
| --- | --- |

Creating Your Own "Templates" .............................. 110

Creating Master ........................................................ 111

## Sharing and Exporting Documents ...................... 112

Syncing Documents with iCloud............................... 113

Emailing a Document From Pages ........................... 113

Collaborating ........................................................... 113

Export a Pages Document ....................................... 114

Printing ................................................................... 115

## Understanding Accessibility On the mac............. 117

Vision ...................................................................... 118

Media ...................................................................... 118

Hearing ................................................................... 119

Interacting ............................................................... 119

Voice Control .......................................................... 120

## Appendix: Keyboard Shortcuts ............................ 121

General Keyboard Shortcuts ................................... 121

Formatting Keyboard Shortcuts............................... 123

## About the Author .................................................. 126

**Disclaimer**: Please note, while every effort has been made to ensure accuracy, this book is not endorsed by Apple, Inc. and should be considered unofficial.

# Introduction

Pages is powerful software, and if you get a Mac, it's free. But let's face it: you've probably spent most of your life using Word—or if you were a renegade, WordPerfect.

For a Mac user, Pages can make your documents really shine…but first you need to know how to use it. This guide will help!

Instead of spending hundreds of pages on functions you probably will never use, it shows you what you really want to know: the basics.

In no time, you'll be creating visually stunning documents!

It will show you the ropes—including how to do all those things you are used to doing in Microsoft Word-and help you with some of the features you may not even know about.

Ready to get started? Let's go!

Note: This guide is based off of the bestselling series *The Ridiculously Simple Guide to Pages For Mac*. It has an added section on accessibility.

# [1]

## Understanding Word Processing On Your Mac

This chapter will cover:
- How to get Pages
- Opening your first document
- Pages crash course
- Formatting text
- Layouts and styles

### How To Get Pages

Depending on how you acquired your Mac, you may or may not have Pages already. Getting it is easy. And even better: getting it is free! (you can see if you have it by going into the Launchpad from the dock and searching for Pages).

There's one catch: not all Macs are supported. But most are. MacOS 10.14 is required to run Pages, which means you must have one of the following computers:
- MacBook: Early 2015 or newer
- MacBook Air: Mid 2012 or newer
- MacBook Pro: Mid 2012 or newer
- Mac Mini: Late 2012 or newer
- iMac: Late 2012 or newer
- iMac Pro
- Mac Pro: Late 2013 or newer; Mid 2010 or Mid 2012 models require a Metal-capable GPU

As long as you have one of those, then you can go to the App Store (it's in your Launchpad). Pages is a digital download only—you cannot obtain a physical copy of it. The download is a few hundred MB.

From there, type in Pages in the search, and hit the return key.

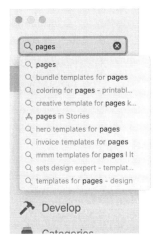

If you have it, the return result will have an Open button; if you don't have it, the result will show a Get button. When you click Get, you'll be prompted to put in your Apple ID and password; if you don't have an Apple ID, then follow the on-screen instructions to get one (this is free).

## Running Pages for the First Time

When you first open Pages, you'll be asked if you want to use iCloud. I recommend you do; this makes it easy to save and open documents across all devices—if you are writing a document on your phone, for instance, you can open that document and continue working on it from your tablet—it's all very seamless and doesn't require anything extra on your part once it's set up.

If you set up iCloud, you can even access and type documents right in your browser—there's nothing else to install on your computer, which means "technically" you could use Pages on a Windows computer or even a Chromebook or Android device—I'll show you how at the end of this chapter.

## The Pages Crash Course

The first time you use Pages, you'll get a brief tutorial. You can either watch it or skip it.

Each time you open Pages, you'll be greeted with a directory box that asks you if you want to open a document or if you want to create a new one. We'll be working off a new document in this chapter, so click "New Document" in the lower left corner.

The next box you'll see is all the available templates you can use. A template is a premade document that you can add text into. For example, if you want to write a resume, you can use the resume Template, and you would just keep the formatting but type over the text that's there with the text that matches you. Templates are listed under categories.

If you don't want to start with a template, then click on the first option (which says Blank).

First time users of Pages are often a little disappointed the first time they use Pages; if you've Word, then you have ribbons and menus and options everywhere! Pages looks pretty bare next to that.

Don't worry—looks can be deceiving; there are plenty of options when you know how to find them, and I'll show you each of them in this book.

If you feel overwhelmed already because there are options, you can hide that side panel by clicking on the Format button in the upper right corner.

Now that you have a blank screen, let's go over the very basics of Pages.

### Select

To select a single word, move your mouse over it and click twice.

### Select Paragraph

To select all words in the paragraph, click three times over any word in the paragraph you want to select.

### Select All

Select All selects everything in your document. It's a very powerful command! It brings up the same options as Select, but any changes you make will be applied to the entire document.

To Select All, use Command + A on your keyboard.

## Select Options

Now that you have the text selected, what do you do? If you click with two fingers on your trackpad or mouse, then the options box comes up. We'll go over what these options are as we continue in the book.

## Cut, Copy and Paste

To copy and paste words (and images, tables and charts) quicker, you can use keyboard shortcuts.

Selecting content and hitting COMMAND + C will copy it.

Selecting content and hitting COMMAND + X will cut it.

And hitting COMMAND + V will copy the content anywhere you want it in the document.

## Find and Replace

Find and Replace is a handy little feature in Pages that allows you to replace your selection with alternatives

Let's say you just wrote the opening chapter to your first book. But once you are done, you realize you want your character to be a 'her' instead of a 'him,' and you want to replace all of the "he said" with "she said." It can be done in seconds!

Go to edit from your menu bar, and select Find > Find.

From here you can find all the uses of the word you want to find, but you can also click the down arrow on the left side and select Find & Replace. This lets you search for a word (top line) and replace the word once it finds it (bottom line). When you have both the find and replace word added, then you can click Replace & Find.

## Define

Pages has a handy little dictionary built in. You can select any word, tap the trackpad twice to bring up the options menu, and tap Look Up to see the definition of any word.

The dictionary will give you multiple definitions (and a thesaurus); even more, you can select options at the bottom to see movies related to the word, Siri Knowledge (which is encyclopedic information), apps related to it, and more!

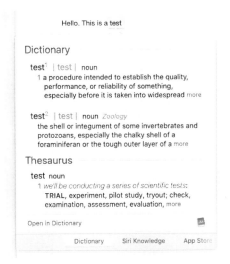

## Copy Style

The Style command lets you copy and paste styles, like the Microsoft Word format painter feature. If you ever want to make a piece of text look like another, just select the text with the format you'd like to copy, click Format > Copy Style; then select the text you want to alter and click Format > Paste Style. This can be a major time saver!

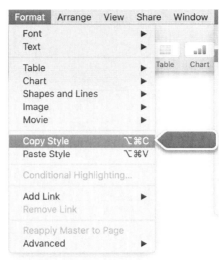

INSERTING HYPERLINKS

If you want to insert a hyperlink to an internet resource, just type out the link. Pages automatically detects hyperlinks and will insert the link for you. To edit the link or to change the displayed text, just click the link and then tap Link Settings. Here you can edit the link itself, change the text displayed, or remove the link altogether.

If you aren't typing a web address, but want to link it to a web address (for example, you are typing: "I go to UCLA" and you want to provide a hyperlink to UCLA), then select the word you want to hyperlink and click with two fingers to bring up the options. From here, just click Add Link and select the kind of link you want to add. You can edit and remove it the same way as in the previous paragraph.

Undo/Redo

If you mess up (for example you delete a paragraph that you shouldn't have) you can Undo it by going to Edit > Undo; you can also redo it under the same menu.

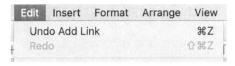

## Hands-On Exercise

This exercise will help you familiarize yourself with the commands we've covered in this section. Just follow the steps below, referring to the above if needed.

Open a blank document.

Type the sentence "The quick brown fox jumps over the lazy dog."

Select the entire sentence.

Copy the sentence.

Tap Enter to start a new line.

Paste the sentence.

In the second sentence, select the word "brown" and replace it with your favorite iPad suggestion.

In the second sentence, add a Phonetics guide to the entire sentence for English learners in the language of your choice (use the guide of your choice). Hint: this sentence can be selected with a triple tap!

Your document should now look like this:

## The Formatting Toolbar

There are a few menu options to work with in Pages, but in this section, we will be covering the Formatting Toolbar, which is on the right side of your document.

Under Text, it will say "Body" by default. When you click it, you'll see several options. "Body" is normal text in a document—the text you are reading right here would be considered Body Text. Documents have several types of paragraph text; for example, each section of this chapter has a

"Heading"—you could just change the font size and make it "look" like a heading, but using a Paragraph Style tells Pages what kind of text it is so it can put together a table of contents later.

Some of the styles will not be very common, "Label Dark" for example.

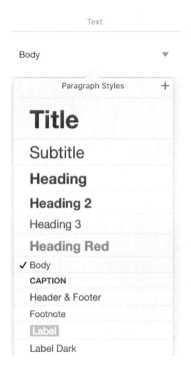

Under this is options for Style, Layout, and More. Let's stay on Style for now, so the next option is Font.

It says 11pt Helvetica; this is the font. If you tap on it, you'll be able to select a new font and adjust the size. Pages offers a healthy font selection, including perennial favorites like Arial, Times New

Roman, and Helvetica. Some notable absences include Comic Sans (and yet Papyrus still made the cut), Calibri, and Cambria.

The "regular" dropdown shows you all the style choices for that font (some fonts have different options).

The next three buttons are fairly standard. If you're not familiar with computerized word processing, though, remember B for Bold, I for Italic, and U for underline. The S with a line through it puts a strike across any text you type.

Below this are your alignment buttons. Tap them for options to align your text left, center or right, or justify it. Justified text is text that fills one line exactly. Try it out to see how it works.

The next two buttons are indent buttons. Use them to indent, or to move backwards through indents.

Finally, below this is where you can add bulleted lists and line spacing (if you want to double space, for example).

### Hands-On Exercise

This is exercise will help you practice with all of the formatting options available to you in the formatting toolbar.

Type up a heading and a few lines of text in a blank Pages document (you can also use your "quick brown fox" document from the previous exercise if you prefer).

Change your heading so that it appears in Georgia, 20 pt. font, bold, and underlined. Center the heading.

Change the text under the heading so that it is right aligned and italicized.

More Formatting Options in Styles

## Layout

The Layout menu lets you put text into columns and adjust line spacing. Yes, you can use Pages to draft that paper for your picky professor who insists on 1.25 spacing (click indents)!

You can also use layout to create columns (if you are writing a newsletter, for example).

## More

The More option is what you will use for pagination and hyphenation.

## Pagination & Breaks
☐ Keep lines on same page
☐ Keep with next paragraph
☐ Start paragraph on a new page
☑ Prevent widow & orphan lines

## Hyphenation & Ligatures
☐ Remove paragraph hyphenation
☐ Remove ligatures

**Following Paragraph Style**
Same

## OPENING PAGES FROM iCLOUD

Pages can be run right from your browser; it's great for editing, but for intensive design work, the best solution will be your computer.

To access it from your browser, head to iCloud.com and sign in with your Apple ID.

The first screen you'll see will show you all the things you can do from the cloud; one of them is using Pages. Click it once to open it.

As long as you've been saving your work to the cloud, then any recent docs will show up here, and you can click on their thumbnail once to open them.

You can additionally start a new Doc by clicking on the + button in the upper right corner. This will open up Pages for iCloud. All the features covered in this book can be found in Pages for iCloud as well.

## Managing Documents

Saving in Pages is pretty straightforward—especially if you've used Windows before. It's under File > Save.

30 | *Pages for Mac*

Before we move forward with using other features in Pages, I want to go over the less straightforward ways to manage documents.

### Renaming Documents

Renaming documents is very easy. Like with many things in Pages, there's more than one way to do it.

The easiest way is when your document is open; just click on the name in the top center of the document.

The next way is File > Rename.

The third way is to find it in Finder, click with two fingers, and select Rename.

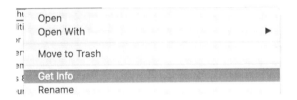

## Hands-On Exercise

These exercises are going to get progressively more challenging! Ready to try your hand at some serious formatting?

Open up a blank Pages document.

Copy and paste a chunk of text from somewhere else (I used the Lorem Ipsum generator at lipsum.org to get five paragraphs of filler text).

> Hint: you can visit a webpage and copy text the same way you would in Pages. Then, go back to Pages and paste.

Format it so that it displays as 14 pt., justified, bold, double-spaced red Arial.

Format your text so that it is displayed in three columns. (Remember Columns is under layout.)

| Lorem ipsum dolor sit amet, consectetur adipiscing elit. Sed at vestibulum erat. Donec nisl metus, dignissim sed hendrerit ut, congue quis nibh. Nulla nec elit leo, in tempus | imperdiet urna nec facilisis. Duis vitae libero a urna feugiat egestas sit amet eu sem. Vestibulum gravida aliquam tortor, ut porta augue varius sed. Maecenas ac massa | Fusce sit amet placerat magna. Pellentesque tempor euismod metus quis varius. Sed et odio nec lectus bibendum molestie. Sed vehicula libero eget quam interdum |

# [2]
## ADDING / EDITING PHOTOS IN PAGES

This chapter will cover:
- Insert image
- Arrange / Rotate / Wrap image
- Edit Mask / Alpha
- Image Styling

As much as possible, I'm trying to make learning Pages fun; there's no better way to make something fun than with photos!

As we go, we'll be learning more about styling tips, but before we get there, we are going to learn about photos—not just about inserting them into the document, but about how to apply more advanced techniques to them.

## INSERTING AN IMAGE

Inserting an image can be done several ways. You can copy and paste an image into the document, you can drag a photo into the document, or you can pick it manually.

To pick it manually, you can go to Insert > Choose, and then find the file location.

The quicker way to add a photo, however, is from the menu. Click the image button, which shows you all the different media types you can add. Why would it show movies and music? You can't exactly print those out, right? It shows these options because Pages lets you create interactive electronic documents. This section will focus on photos, however. You can get photos by clicking on Photos or Image Gallery (if the photos are in your gallery) or by clicking "Choose" to pick where the photo is located.

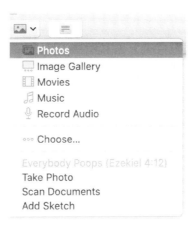

If you pick photos, it's not going to show you all of your photos—just the photos in that photos area of your Mac. You could, for example, have a photo on your USB drive. If that's the case, then you'd want to pick "Choose" from the previous menu instead of photos.

## Arranging Images

### Resize and Rotate

Once your image is inserted, you can use your mouse to move it, resize it, and rotate it. Resizing is pretty straightforward. Click the image, then move to the corner or side of the image and move the little squares on the edges in and out. To rotate the image you'll do the same thing, but when you get to the corner of the image, press the Command key on your keyboard. This will show you a curved line and also show you the percentage of the rotation as you move the image.

Hint: Looking for images? I often use a website named pexels.com to find public domain (or free to use images).

There's one more way to rotate an image. When you click on the image, you'll notice that the side panel that you used to format text has changed. It's now a new menu with controls to format an image.

There are three buttons on top of this menu (Style, Image, Arrange); we'll go over the first button in the next section, but for this section, go to Arrange.

On the bottom of this menu, there's a section called Rotate; angle is what you want to use. The mouse is a quick and easy way to rotate your image, but if you want precision, then this is the best method. Next to the Angle button, you can also vertically and horizontally flip the image using the arrows.

### Text Wrap and Placement

Let's go back up to the top of the image arrange menu; the first thing you see is Object Placement. The default is Move with Text; this means as you add text above the image, the image moves down. Stay on page means you want it locked into place on the page and it won't move—this is commonly used for watermarks.

Below this is the Text Wrap. Automatic is the default setting, but if you click on it, you'll notice several other options.

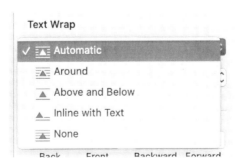

The default option has text above or below the object.

If you want text to wrap around the image, then just click Around.

Notice the white space around the image is kind of tight? If you want it more squared off, then go below the text wrap to Text Fit and you can make it more even with the toggle.

Text Fit

The example below uses the first option under fit.

The next set of options let you pick the size of the image; again, you can do this manually with your mouse, but this lets you be a little more precise.

Finally, the last option lets you pick the placement of the image—if you want it in the middle of the page, for example.

Earlier, I said you could make an image a watermark; great! But you'll notice the options that let you move the image back / forward are greyed out. So how do you make a watermark if you can't move the object behind the text?

Back    Front    Backward  Forward

It's tricky. The current mode we are using is Word Processing mode. It's much easier to edit and get everything to align right, but options like these will be missing. To make a watermark, we need it to be in Page Layout mode. We can convert it, but we'll lose all of our text, unfortunately.

To convert it, go to File > Convert to Page Layout.

The image can now be moved to the back, but here's the big drawback. Text is now in a text box (see below). That makes dealing with margins and new pages a lot harder. This mode is great for things like fliers; not so good for lengthy documents. So you're out of luck? Not exactly. I'll show you how to add watermarks in a better way later in this chapter.

IMAGE GROUPING

There's one last section that's greyed out. Grouping. Grouping is greyed out because you need two images to use it.

Add a second image, then click the image, press command on your keyboard and select the second image; the Group option is no longer greyed out. What grouping does is put two images together, so that when you edit the size, rotation, etc., you are treating the two photos as one image.

Text.Sample Text.Sample Text.Sample Text.Sample Text.Sample Text

If you want to edit just one image, you don't have to ungroup it. You can double click the image to tell Pages that you want to keep them grouped, but you want to make changes to one photo while they are grouped.

## Watermarks

Earlier, we saw how you couldn't send an object to the background to create a watermark without converting it to Page Layout mode. So that means a word processing document can't have a watermark, right? Nope!

You can create a watermark with something called Section Masters. Once you make all the changes you want to the image and have it where you want it to go, go to Arrange > Section Masters > Move Object to Section Master. It's now a watermark and every new page will show the image.

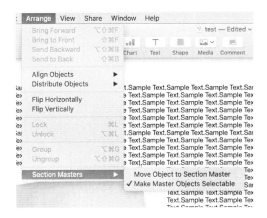

E<small>DIT</small> M<small>ASK AND</small> A<small>LPHA</small>

With your image selected (note: if the images are grouped, you need to double click the image you want to edit—you can't edit both images at the same time), select the Image button.

This brings up options for image enhancements. At the bottom is the Adjustments section; this section is pretty self-explanatory - the Exposure and Saturation sliders will change the amount of exposure / saturation in the image. The Enhance button will do an auto enhancement based on what the computer thinks the image should look like (the reset button will undo it).

Next to the Enhance button is a control button; this will bring up more adjustment controls.

Most people probably won't need this many controls, but it's helpful to know it's there.

The section that may not be as easy to understand is the top section: Edit Mask and Instant Alpha.

Edit Mask is essentially an image crop. You can use this to cut off parts of the image without resizing it.

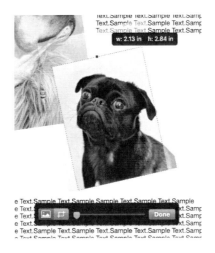

Instant Alpha is one of my personal favorite image editing tools. It removes the background of the image. It's great when your image has a very solid background (you're standing against a solid color wall, for example).

One you click on it, the cursor turns to a square box and you click and drag over the areas you want to take out.

As you click, the sections that are removed will turn a different color to indicate what has been removed. When you're done, let go of the mouse and click the done button.

As you remove the background, it is also auto-cropping; so if you've removed the background from the top, the image has automatically been cropped to accommodate for it.

STYLING YOUR IMAGE

Now that we know how to move an image around, let's add some style to it.

To style your image, tap the image. Style is the first button on the image edit menu.

## Basic Styles

The top box lets you add quick, pre-defined image styles to your image. For example, if you want your image to have a box around it.

Most people will probably want to do manual editing to the photo, but if you use the arrow in this section, you'll notice a + button. Once you manually make changes to the image (add your transparency, borders, etc.), you can use this button to save these changes, so you can apply them to another photo that you want to have a similar look and feel.

Image Styles

## BORDER

The next section is the Border; there is no border on the image by default. If you click the box with the red diagonal line, it will show a drop down of all the different styles available.

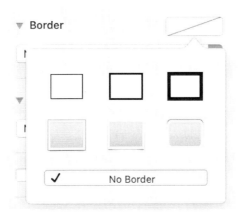

Once you pick your border style, you be able to adjust the weight of the border using the slider.

If you click the preview of the border, you will also see all the different border styles for the style that you have picked. Styles vary depending on the style you are using.

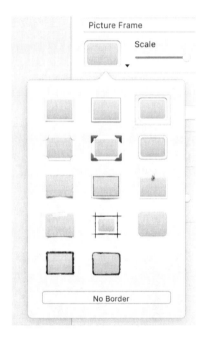

### Shadow

Shadows can add a little more dimension to your photo and help it pop off the page more. It works very similar to Borders; click the thumbnail with the red line through it, then pick the shadow style.

Once you pick the style, you'll get several shadow options to increase or decrease the amount of shadowing used.

As you make changes, the image will change in real-time, so you immediately see the effects. Notice in the image below how the image has a more 3D look?

### Reflection

Reflection is a simple check / uncheck box; you can use the slider to adjust the amount of reflection used, but that's the only edit available.

You can see in the example below how the reflection gave the image the appearance of an image reflecting on the page (the reflection is the darker area on the bottom of the image).

## Transparency

The final style change is transparency. Transparency makes an image more see-through (see the example below). This is great for something like a watermark, but doesn't help a lot if you don't have something below the image.

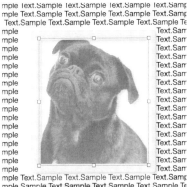

In the below example, I put the transparent image above another photo to illustrate how you can use it on top of another image.

HANDS-ON EXERCISE

1. Insert an image into a blank document (or copy and paste the image from the Internet using Command C and Command V).
2. Give the image a special Photo Corners border (or a border of your choosing).
3. Give the image a large, fuzzy shadow.
4. Give the image a 76% reflection.
5. Set the image opacity to 68%.
6. Resize the image so that you can see the full image and its reflection without scrolling.

Your screen should now look something like this:

# [3]
# Inserting and Formatting Tables

This chapter will cover:
- Inserting a table
- Styling a table
- Deleting a table
- Importing a table

Pages works seamlessly with other iWork apps like Numbers and Keynote; this is especially true with tables. You can insert tables into your document manually, but you can also import tables from Numbers into it. This section will show you how and will also serve as a brief introduction to Numbers for the iPad.

## Inserting a Table

If you have ever added a table in Word, then you may be used to picking the size and width before adding the table; in Pages, you add the table and then adjust it accordingly.

To add a table, tap the Table button from the top menu bar (you can also use Insert > Table from the menu options at the top of MacOS). You'll have several styles to pick from, but again, this is different from Word where you drag to the number of rows and columns that you want.

### Adding Columns and Rows

Your table is now inserted, but chances are it's not the right size.

At the bottom of the last row (or the side of the last column) there's a circle with two lines. Click on either of those to adjust the number of columns / rows. You can either use the up / down arrows to pick, or you can click the number and then type the amount you want.

INTERACTING WITH TABLES

It can be a little tricky to work with a table in Pages at first. Double clicking a cell will bring up the keyboard, but single clicking it will select the entire cell (Microsoft Excel users should have an easier time with this concept).

If there's no text, you can single click and start typing, but if you want to edit the text that's already there, then you need to double click.

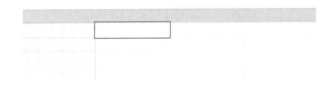

## Row / Column Options

If you want to delete or add a row / column, then go to the row or column you want to make changes to, and then click the drop-down arrow. Several options will come up.

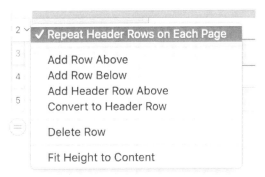

You can also click the number associated with the row / column to select all. This is helpful if you want to copy / paste a row or column.

## Styling Tables

Apple's predefined tables look great, but if you've got a specific color scheme or style in mind, it's easy to customize your tables to match that. Just select your table (or certain cells in your table) and look to the right side menu, which has changed to a table style menu.

### Table Options

The first set of options are for the entire table.

These are all options that would change everything in the table. Such as the table outline; if you can see grids and alternating row colors (if you want row 1 white, row 2 black, row 3 white, row 4 black, etc.). You can also increase the font size and add new rows and columns.

The Table Styles at the top are similar to the image styles; they're predefined styles.

CELL OPTIONS

The table options are great if you want to change everything about the table. But what if you just want to change a cell, column, or row? That's where the Cell Option tab comes into play.

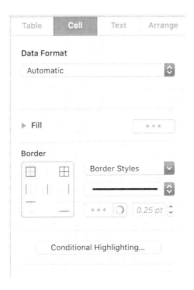

It says "Cell" but Cell here is anything that you highlight. So if you highlight one cell, then it's just that cell; but if you highlight multiple cells, then it's each of those cells.

Data Format is where you can change what is inside the cell; what does that mean? Let's say one of your columns had only currency; you could highlight that column and then say that everything in those cells were currency; so a dollar sign would be added to all the numbers in the cells.

You can change the color of the cell under Fill; you can change the border style, border color, and border weight under Border.

Conditional Highlighting is a little less obvious than those first couple of options.

This lets you create rules; for example anytime you have a cell with the number 2, the cell text turns Bold.

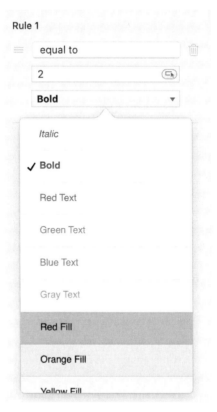

## Text Options

By now you should understand how to format text. It's no different when you are doing a table. The same rules as before apply—any cell you highlight will have the text changed—so if you have the entire row highlighted, then all the text in those cells changes.

There is one box worth noting: Wrap text in cell. It's just a check / uncheck box, but it's important because if you have a long string of text and you want it to fit within a cell without going into the next cell, then you need it to wrap.

Here's an example of wrapping off.

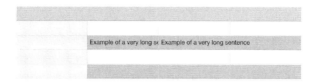

And here's what it looks like on.

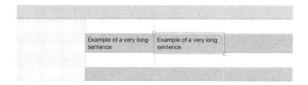

ARRANGE OPTIONS

Just like text options are the same as formatting options outside of the table, Arrange Options are almost identical to the options covered in Photo Arrangement options.

DELETING TABLES

Deleting an entire table is a quick process. Click the table. Hit delete.

## Importing Tables

Importing a table from somewhere else can be done a few different ways.

The first, and quickest, way is to copy and paste the table. Command V is obviously the easiest way to do this, but go to the Edit menu. Notice there are a Paste and Paste and Match Styles options? If you aren't getting the paste results that you want, try this Paste instead.

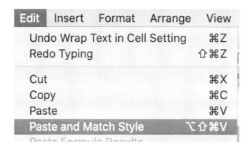

If you don't need to make changes to the table, what a lot of people prefer to do is just make a screenshot of the spreadsheet: Command + Shift + 3 (or Command + Shift + 4 if you want to do only select areas of the screen).

## Hands-on Exercise

This one's a little more of a challenge!
1. Insert a table with the style of your choice.
2. Adjust the table so that it contains three rows and three columns (including headers)

3. Enter labels for each row and column and numerical data in each cell.
4. Select your bottom row and copy it.
5. Add an additional row.
6. Paste your copied row into the new row.
7. Select the whole table and turn alternating rows on.
8. Turn on Header Row Lines.
9. Change the Table Font to Arial.
10. Select your column headers. Change them to a green fill with blue bold underlined text centered in the middle of the cell and right aligned.

Now your screen should look something like this:

|       | Column 1 | Column 2 |
|-------|----------|----------|
| Row 1 | 1        | 2        |
| Row 2 | 3        | 4        |
| Row 2 | 3        | 4        |

# [4]
## INSERTING / FORMATTING CHARTS

This chapter will cover:
- Inserting a Chart
- Editing Chart Data
- Styling a Chart

Charts can add color and interest to your documents, as well as help you present data more clearly. Pages includes a powerful Charts feature that allows you to quickly create beautiful, customizable charts that really pop out of the page.

Now that you know how to use Tables, using Charts will be a breeze.

## Inserting a Chart

To insert a chart in Pages, tap the Insert button, then tap Charts. From here, you'll choose the type of chart (bar, area, line, pie), as well as the style you want. Choose from several different color schemes in 2D, 3D, and interactive. If you change your mind about your chart choice, you can always change it later, without losing any data you've entered. Just tap on your favorite chart to insert it into your document.

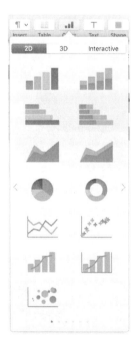

As with almost everything in Pages, you can also add Charts from the top menu (Insert > Chart).

Once you have your chart picked, a chart that's already filled out will be added to your document (I'm using a Pie chart in this chapter, but the same features apply to almost all of the charts—they just look a little different).

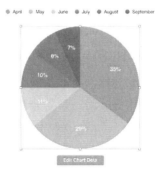

## Editing Chart Data

It's so nice for Pages to put a pretty chart that's all filled out into our document, right? Sure! But wouldn't it be nicer if it had meaningful data? To add your own data, click Edit Chart Data. This brings up a mini table that you can edit with whatever information you want.

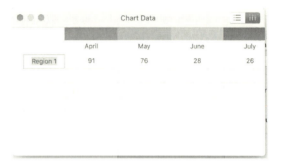

I'm going to replace the months with the names of states, and use an entirely different data range. The chart changes with each change I make in the table. Notice that the chart below is completely different from the one above?

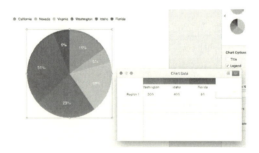

You can enter additional rows if you need to—but this won't work on all charts (like the pie chart).

## STYLING YOUR PIE CHART

Now that you have the data you want, it's time to style it.

If you did a pie chart, then you'll see three options on the side (Chart, Wedges, Arrange).

Other charts (like bar charts) have four (Chart, Axis, Series, Arrange).

I'll go over the two extra options for a bar chart in the next section.

In the Chart section you can make changes to the entire chart. By default the chart has no title, but if you check off the box, a title (cleverly named "Title") is added to your chart; you'll probably want to name it something else. To do that (and this also applies to renaming pretty much anything in your chart) double click on it and start typing.

Below the title is where you can change the font, and under that, the chart colors. When you click on the chart colors, it gives you a whole host of pre-defined colors. But what if you want to pick your own?

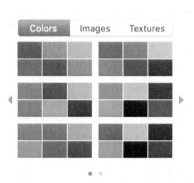

There's one extra small step to picking your own colors. You have to double click on the wedge that you want to change the color of, and then over on the menu options to the right of it, click Style (Style is a new option that's only there if you double click the wedge). From here, you can pick a color under "Fill."

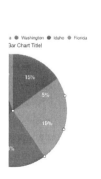

While we are in this section, let's go just under it to Stroke and Shadow. Both of these options help a wedge stand out a little. This is useful if you want to illustrate one area of the chart over others. See in the example below how I added a dotted line (and increased the line weight to 4) and also added a shadow.

If you really want that wedge to stand out, try pulling it apart from the chart. You can do that by clicking on the Wedge option, and then changing the Wedge Position. Look at the example below; the wedge is now separated in the chart.

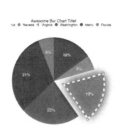

Now let's go back to the chart section and look at the other options we can apply to the entire chart. You can give it a background, add a shadow to it, and finally, change the Chart Type. You can make it a different Pie chart or turn it into a line chart (note: this will probably interfere with your data and you may have to redo some of it).

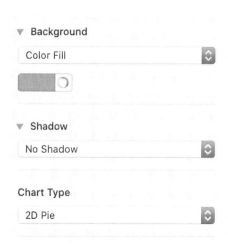

We saw how going to the Wedge section could separate your single wedge from the rest. If you don't double click the wedge and change it, below is what happens.

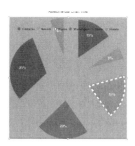

All the wedges separate. If that's what you want, then perfect! If that's not what you want, undo and then double click the wedge you want to separate.

Checking off Data Point Names will put the names of the value in chart (you can also keep it in the Legend).

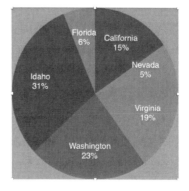

The values on the chart are currently shown as percentages; if you prefer showing them as numbers (or another value type), you can change this under Value Format.

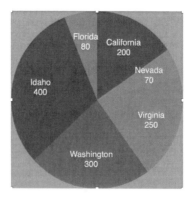

If you check off Lender Lines, you probably won't notice a difference; to see what the lines are, click the Straight drop-down and change it to Angled.

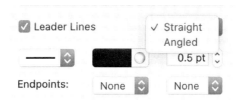

You should now see lines to the sides of the chart.

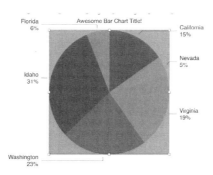

The arrange option should look familiar to you. You've seen it in the Tables section and the Photos section; it's the same features.

## Styling Your Bar Chart

Now that you know how to style a Pie Chart, you'll have no problem with the Bar Chart; it's basically the same, but with more options for labels.

In the axis sub-tab, you can turn category labels, series names, gridlines, and titles on and off. Similarly, in the Y-axis or X-axis sub-tab, you can turn value labels, gridlines, and titles on and off. Here you can also specify the number format you'd like to use and adjust the value scale settings. Number formatting includes the option to add prefixes and suffixes, like currency symbols or suffixes like %, millions, etc.

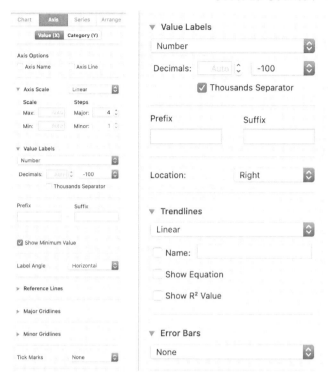

Note: the contents of the sub-tabs change depending on the orientation of your chart. The number formatting option may appear under either the x- or y-axis, depending on the type of chart you've inserted.

## Hands-On Exercise

Let's create a chart! Create a chart with the following specifications:
1. Insert a 3D bar chart.
2. Edit the data so that it shows how much money Company A and Company B

made in the years 2010, 2011, and 2012 (amounts are up to you!).
3. Show gridlines on the chart for both the x and y-axis.
4. Give the chart the title "Profits of Company A and Company B."
5. Give the category axis the title "Year" and the value axis the title "Profits."
6. Remember that the x and y axes depend on what orientation your bar chart is in.
7. Give the value axis value labels a dollar sign prefix and a K suffix.
8. Change the shape of the bars to cylinders.

Your screen should now look something like this:

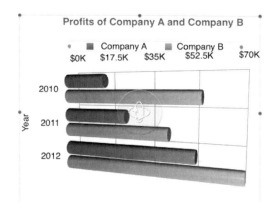

# [5]
## CREATING SHAPES

This chapter will cover:
- Inserting a Shape
- Resizing Shapes
- Creating Text Boxes

Pictures are great! They really help your document look snazzy. But there's one more type of graphical illustration you should consider: shapes. Shapes can be great additions to a document – they can be used to draw attention to an area of a document or to illustrate your points graphically. Pages offers a number of handy pre-made shapes for you to use, and I'll show you how to get the most out of them.

## Inserting a Shape

To insert a shape into a document, click the shape button or go to Insert > Shape from the top menu. This will bring up all the shapes available for you. Find the one you like and click it to insert it.

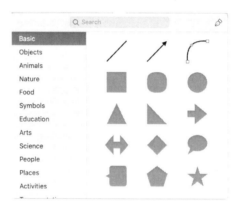

Remember that you can change the color, border and shadow/reflection effects later!

Shapes sounds a little misleading. If you're like me, you're probably thinking square, circle, etc. But shapes in Pages are kind of like clipart. Yes, basic shapes are there, but so are other things. In the example below I searched for "Dog" and got five results!

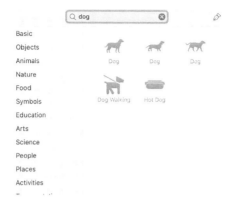

## Resizing Shapes and Adjusting Proportions

Shape resizing is just like resizing photos: tap on a corner and drag it to the desired size. However, with Shapes, you can also adjust proportions. What does that mean? It's better shown than explained. Double tap your trackpad on the shape to bring up the shape options. Now click "Make Editable."

There's now a bunch of dots on the shape. These represent points that you can adjust.

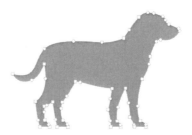

As an example, I moved the point inward from the dog's stomach and look what happened.

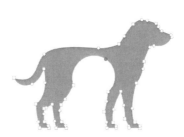

By default you make these changes with a curved point, but you can change this by bringing the options up again. Notice the three different points?

### MOVING AND ROTATING SHAPES

To move a shape, simply tap on it and drag it to a new location. To rotate a shape, click the image then press the command button—just like you would an image.

### ADDING TEXT TO A SHAPE

To add text on top of a shape, double-tap on it to activate its text field. Then just type your text!

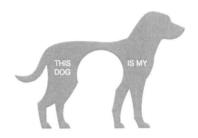

### CREATING TEXT BOXES

There's one more type of shape, but it's not under shape. It's a Text Box. Text Boxes are exactly what they sound like—floating boxes that have text.

Why use a Text Box instead of typing out the text? Ideally, you want to use them when you are making something like a title—not when you are typing out your epic novel. It's for short text that you want to stand out.

Unlike standard text, Text Boxes are treated in the same way images are, so you can easily move them around and have other things wrap around them.

To get started, click the T in the menu.

You can also do Insert > Text Box.

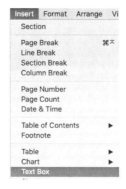

This puts a floating box with generic text in your document.

You can change the color of the box and more by clicking on Style; it has all the same types of options that you'd find in the Image or Shape options.

Because it's a Shape, you are able to edit it like you would a shape. In the below example, I curved out the bottom portion of the box.

## Styling Shapes and Text Boxes

Styling Shapes and Text boxes is the same as styling an image, so I won't repeat myself here. If you are confused about styling, referred to the section in the Photos chapter.

## Hands-On Exercise

Let's practice using shapes and text boxes. Follow the directions below.
1. Insert two shapes of your choice.
2. Make one shape blue with a gradient and texture. Give it a solid 1 px black border. Add a shadow effect and reduce its opacity to 50%.
3. Make the other shape red with a gradient. Add a shadow effect.
4. Add text to each shape – make one read "Blue" and the other "Red."
5. Make the text white, underlined, and in Marker Felt typeface. Hint: don't forget about copying and pasting styles!

Now your screen should look something like this.

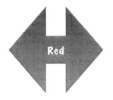

# [6]
## Setting Up a Document

This chapter will cover:
- Change margins
- Custom paper size
- Headers / Footers
- Bookmarks
- Table of contents
- Track changes

For most documents, using the preset template will do the job; for those who need a bit more customization, there is Document Setup (for Word users, this is kind of like Page Setup); here you will be able to adjust margins, headers and footers).

## Entering Document Setup Mode

To use Document Setup, you can go to View > Inspector > Document Setup.

You can also use the Format / Document toggle icons in the menu bar to switch between them.

This brings up your main document editor with three tab options: Document, Section, Bookmarks.

## Changing Document Margins and Size

In Document Setup, the settings that pertain to margins and paper size are all found in the first tab: Document.

At the top of the settings, under Printer and Paper Size, you can see all the different paper sizes available. Keep in mind that changing to a different printer may give you more (or less) sizes.

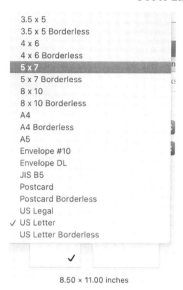

Below this, you can change the orientation of the paper from portrait to landscape.

Finally, you can change the margins under Document Margins. One inch all around is the default setting.

To change the margins, go to Document Setup, then drag the margins to where you would like them to go. Tap "Done" when you are finished.

CREATING CUSTOM PAPER SIZE

What about if you don't see your size? You can create a custom size, but keep in mind if you are printing the document, it may not print correctly.

To create a custom size, go to File > Page Setup.

98 | Pages for Mac

Next, click the drop down under Paper Size.

Finally, add your custom size.

## Hyphenations and Ligatures

At the bottoms of Document Setup are two checkboxes: Hyphenations and Ligatures. Checking them turns them on and off.

Hyphenation puts a dash next to long words at the end of the page margin—the idea is to make the document look more even by breaking up a word and continuing it on the next line.

>le text. This is sample
s sample text. This is
t. This is sample text.
iple text. This is sam-
is sample text. This is
t. This is sample text.

Ligatures are two letters that are combined together to create one character. See some examples below.

$$AE \rightarrow \text{Æ}$$
$$ae \rightarrow \text{æ}$$
$$OE \rightarrow \text{Œ}$$
$$oe \rightarrow \text{œ}$$
$$ff \rightarrow \text{ff}$$
$$fi \rightarrow \text{fi}$$

## Headers and Page Numbers

One of the most useful features of Document Setup Mode is its header and footer options. These document elements will appear on every page of your document. You'll also be able to add page numbers from here.

You can control the size of the Header / Footer in the Document section of Setup.

The placement of the Header / Footer is controlled in Section.

Section lets you tell Pages not to put your Header / Footer on your title page, for example, or to have your numbering start at a certain page.

To insert your Header / Footer, just move your cursor to the top of the page; you'll see a table of sorts with three cells—these represent left, right and center align. You'll also have the option to add the page number to any of these cells.

## BOOKMARKS

Bookmarks are perfect for electronic works. When you add a bookmark it indexes it, and then you can later hyperlink to that bookmark. So you could be on page 2 of a 500 page document, and have it reference a bookmark on page 87; when the user clicks it, it jumps to the section bookmarked.

To create one, highlight the text you want to bookmark, go to the Bookmark tab of Document Setup, and click the Add Bookmark button.

The bookmark is automatically named whatever text you highlighted. So if the text you highlighted says "This is a bookmark" then the bookmark is called "This is a bookmark".

You can single click the name and rename it. This will only change the name of the bookmark and not the text itself.

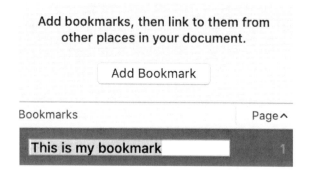

## Table of Contents

If you are working with a document that needs a table of contents, then you first need to make sure you are using the correct headings. Headings tell Pages what will go into the table of contents.

To create a heading, highlight the text you want to be the heading (a chapter title, for example), then go to the format side bar.

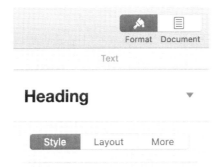

Click the drop down next to Heading and select the type of heading. Heading is usually chapter titles; heading 2 is usually sections; and heading 3 is sections within sections.

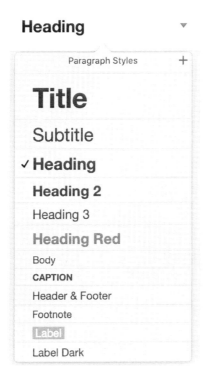

Clicking the arrow next to the heading lets you change how it's formatted; for example, if you want your heading to match the formatting you have, then just click Redefine from Selection.

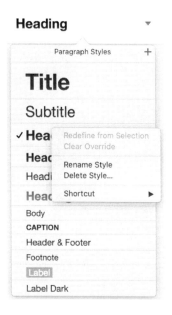

Once you have all the headings in the document, then go to Insert > Table of Contents and select the kind you want. Document is the most common.

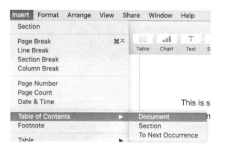

If you click on the inserted table of contents, there will be a table of contents formatter in the format options in the right pane of Pages; you can select what you want to appear in your table of contents here. For example, if you only want Heading 1 to appear, then uncheck everything else.

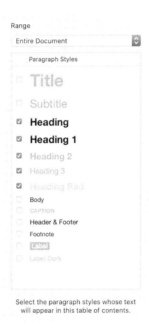

Select the paragraph styles whose text will appear in this table of contents.

## Insert Footnotes

To insert a footnote into your document, highlight the text you want to add a footnote to, then select Insert > Footnote.

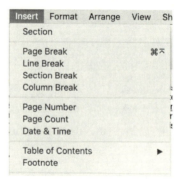

## Insert Comment

If you are editing someone's document and want to add a comment, highlight the sentence you want to add a comment to, right click (or click with two fingers) and add your comment, then click done.

## Track Changes

If you are editing a document, it's also a good idea to turn on Track Changes; this lets the other person see what you have changed.

Track changes is turned on under Edit > Track Changes (it's turned off in the same place).

When it's turned on, a new bar appears at the top of the document, and the color of the changed text is also different. The user now has to accept or reject changes in the document; if they reject them, then the changes go away.

# [7]
# Understanding Templates

> This chapter will cover:
> - Using third-party Pages Templates
> - Creating your own Templates

Pages for iPad comes with over 50 templates in ten categories - some for letters, some for reports and professional use, and others for personal correspondence and announcements.

What exactly is a Template? A Template is a document that's already formatted—complete with text and images. Why would you want that? The idea is you delete the text (and replace the images) to make it your own, but save time on the sometimes complicated formatting aspect of it.

If you are looking for a standard business letter, try "Classic Letter" or "Formal Letter." For a more unusual, offbeat look, you can also try the Personal Photo letter and Modern Photo letters.

Some templates contain multiple pages — for example, a "splashy" front page with enough space for a large photo, followed by more subdued pages for delivering details.

Most of the academic and business-related style templates fall under this category. "Project Proposal," "Term Paper," and "Visual Report" would all be excellent bases with which to start for a highly graphical educational or proposal project.

Pages also includes a party invite, thank you cards, and recipe formats.

Now that you understand most of the formatting options available in Pages, you can use any of these templates as a starting off point. You can change the images, colors, and layout of each template to suit the needs of your project.

## USING THIRD-PARTY PAGES TEMPLATES

50+ templates is a lot, but if you use it long enough, you probably will want a few more; if you get to that place then there are websites (and even apps), which sell Pages templates (sometimes they are free). A basic web search for "Pages templates" or even "free Pages templates" will show you what I mean.

Word of caution: like anything you download, use at your own risk. If a website looks sketchy, be wary of downloading a template.

To use a template like this, just go to the website, find a template you like, follow the site's instructions to download it to your computer's hard drive, and then sync it with your iPad as if it were any other Pages document using the iTunes File Sharing syncing process discussed in "Basic Features."

After that, Pages can open the template and you can begin to edit it. It is strongly recommended to make a duplicate of your template document before you begin working on it, so that you will continue to have a blank one for later if you need it.

These third party templates are great for more variety—for example, if you are looking to give your resume a little more creativity.

## Creating Your Own "Templates"

Unfortunately, Pages currently does not allow you to save templates in the Create New Document screen. However, you can work around this sorely missed feature by setting up your "template" as a regular Pages document.

Personally, I make a duplicate of the document (i.e. File > Duplicate) and name it something like "Resume Template."

CREATING MASTER

If you've created new styles (for example, your headings are X font, size) you can save that as the new default style for all your documents by going to Format > Advanced > Create Master from Current Page.

# [8]
## Sharing and Exporting Documents

> This chapter will cover:
> - Sharing documents
> - Exporting documents

In spite of the popularity of iPhones and iPads, Apple users still often find themselves marooned in a Windows-based world. Pages is a wonderful program, but it's incomprehensible to Microsoft Word. Fortunately, Pages offers several methods for sharing and exporting Pages documents in multiple formats. Pages also makes moving documents across Apple devices absolutely effortless, thanks to iCloud.

## Syncing Documents with iCloud

If you've enabled iCloud in your Pages app, your documents will be synced across your devices automatically, with absolutely no work required on your part. You can even access your documents online from any internet connection at www.icloud.com.

## Emailing a Document From Pages

E-mailing documents is one of the most straightforward methods of sharing your document. Go to Share > Send a Copy.

## Collaborating

You can also collaborate on a document by going to Share > Collaborate With Others.

This brings up an option that asks how you would like the share the document.

I recommend clicking on the Share Options drop down to make sure the right permissions are enabled. For example, you can make the document readable to anyone you share it with or anyone who gets the document; you can also give the user permission to make changes.

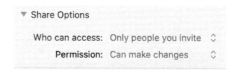

## Export a Pages Document

By default, you'll be saving your file as a .Pages document. That's great if you have Pages, but if you're sharing it with (or opening it on) a computer that doesn't have pages, or you want to create a universal PDF that anyone can see, then you'll need to export it.

This is pretty straightforward. Go to File > Export.

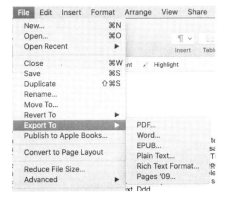

There are six different file types:
- PDF
- Word
- EPUB
- Plain Text
- Rich Text Format
- Pages '09

PDF is the best option if you want to preserve all the formatting in the document and make it look exactly as it appears in Pages. Plain Text will take out all the formatting but be readable on pretty much any editor. ePub is what you would use if you want to create an eBook of your document that can be opened on something like iBooks. Some eReaders don't open ePubs natively and will convert them—so formatting might not be retained.

PRINTING

To print a document, go to File > Print.

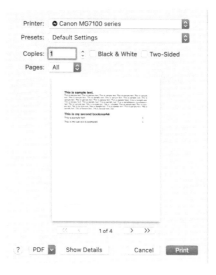

At the bottom of the print menu, there's also an option to save as a PDF. It's Pages' version of Print to File.

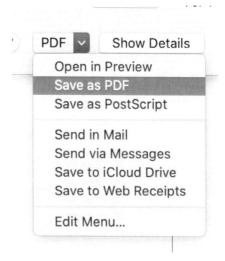

# [9]
## UNDERSTANDING ACCESSIBILITY ON THE MAC

This chapter will cover:
- Sharing documents
- Exporting documents

Accessibility helps you adjust the computer if you have any kind of impairment or disability. It lets you change things like making the display larger, having a voiceover that describes what's on your screen, and put captions on videos when available. This might be helpful for you in Pages.

To open Accessibility, click System Settings and Accessibility. On the left side of the box that comes up will be all the various things you can change. Clicking on each one will create more options.

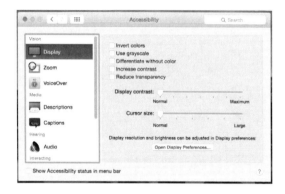

Vision

Under Display, you can make the screen grayscale, invert colors, decrease the contrast, etc. Zoom allows you to create a zoom effect over smaller areas of the screen when you hit a keyboard shortcut. VoiceOver reads back any text that's on the screen.

Media

The Media section includes a few different settings for audio and video playback. Click on Descriptions to enable spoken descriptions for videos.

Captions will apply subtitles and captions to videos.

## Hearing

The Sound tab provides options for the hearing disabled. You can choose to set up a visual flash of the screen each time an alert sound is played, and also decide if you'd like to play stereo audio as mono instead.

## Interacting

Keyboard includes settings for Sticky Keys and Slow Keys. Sticky Keys allows certain buttons to remain activated without you having to hold down the key. For example, if you have Sticky Keys turned on and want to copy some text, instead of holding down Command-C at the same time, you could press the Command button first, followed by the C key. When enabled, you'll hear a lock sound, and any time you use a modifier key like Command, a large icon will appear in the top right corner of the screen indicating that a Sticky Key combination has been started. Slow Keys increases the amount of time between a button press and activation, so if you press Enter, it will take a little longer to actually process.

Mouse & Trackpad features settings like Mouse Keys, which lets you move the mouse around using the number pad on your keyboard, double-click speed, and the option to ignore the built-in Trackpad (on MacBooks) if there is a separate mouse or Trackpad connected to the computer.

Switch Control requires you to enter your administrator password before making any changes, because it's a powerful function that allows you to control the computer using one or more switches that you designate. You can also modify other settings like what to do while navigating, determine pointer precision, and change the size for the Switch Control cursor.

The Dictation tab does exactly what it sounds like—it lets you dictate commands and write or edit text using only your voice. To enable dictation, you first need to click on the bottom button that says Open Dictation & Speech Preferences and selecting the On radio button.

Voice Control

Voice Control lets you control your computer with your voice.

# Appendix: Keyboard Shortcuts

## General Keyboard Shortcuts

| Action | Shortcut |
|---|---|
| Close a window | Command-W |
| Close all windows | Option-Command-W |
| Duplicate a document | Shift-Command-S |
| Enter full-screen view | Control-Command-F |
| Hide or show sidebars on the right side of the Pages window | Option-Command-I |
| Hide or show the toolbar | Option-Command-T |
| Hide Pages | Command-H |
| Hide windows of other applications | Option-Command-H |
| Minimize a window | Command-M |
| Minimize all windows | Option-Command-M |
| Open a new document | Command-N |

| | |
|---|---|
| Open an existing document | Command-O |
| Open the Page Setup window | Shift-Command-P |
| Print a document | Command-P |
| Quit Pages | Command-Q |
| Quit Pages and keep windows open | Option-Command-Q |
| Rearrange an item in the toolbar | Command-drag |
| Redo the last action | Shift-Command-Z |
| Remove an item from the toolbar | Command-drag away from the toolbar |
| Return to actual size | Command-0 |
| Save a document | Command-S |
| Save As | Option-Shift-Command-S |
| Show or hide layout boundaries | Shift-Command-L |
| Show or hide the ruler | Command-R |
| Show or hide the tab bar | Shift-Command-T |
| Show page thumbnails | Option-Command-P |
| Show the Colors window | Shift-Command-C |
| Start dictation | Press Fn twice |
| Undo the last action | Command-Z |

| | |
|---|---|
| Zoom in | Command-Right Angle Bracket (>) |
| Zoom out | Command-Left Angle Bracket (<) |
| Zoom to selection | Shift-Command-0 |

FORMATTING KEYBOARD SHORTCUTS

| Action | Shortcut |
|---|---|
| Show the Fonts window | Command-T |
| Show the Colors window | Shift-Command-C |
| Apply boldface to selected text | Command-B |
| Apply italic to selected text | Command-I |
| Apply underline to selected text | Command-U |
| Make the font size bigger | Command-Plus Sign (+) |
| Make the font size smaller | Command-Minus Sign (-) |
| Make the text superscript | Control-Shift-Command-Plus Sign (+) |
| Make the text subscript | Control-Command-Minus Sign (-) |

| | |
|---|---|
| Insert an equation | Option-Command-E |
| Decrease the indent level of a list item | Shift-Tab |
| Increase the indent level of a list item | Tab |
| Turn text into a link | Command-K |
| Add a bookmark | Option-Command-B |
| Cut the selection | Command-X |
| Copy the selection | Command-C |
| Copy the paragraph style | Option-Command-C |
| Paste the selection | Command-V |
| Paste the paragraph style | Option-Command-V |
| Paste and match the style of the destination text | Option-Shift-Command-V |
| Copy the graphic style of text | Option-Command-C |
| Paste the graphic style of text | Option-Command-V |
| Add a range to (or remove it from) the selection | Shift-drag |
| Insert a nonbreaking space | Option-Space bar |

| | |
|---|---|
| Insert a line break (soft return) | Shift-Return |
| Insert a paragraph break | Return |
| Insert a new line after the insertion point | Control-O |
| Insert a page break | Fn-Command-Return |
| Enter special characters | Control-Command-Space bar |
| Transpose the characters on either side of the insertion point | Control-T |
| Add an EndNote bibliography | Shift-Option-Command-E |

# About the Author

Scott La Counte is a librarian and writer. His first book, *Quiet, Please: Dispatches from a Public Librarian* (Da Capo 2008) was the editor's choice for the Chicago Tribune and a Discovery title for the Los Angeles Times; in 2011, he published the YA book The N00b Warriors, which became a #1 Amazon bestseller; his most recent book is *#OrganicJesus: Finding Your Way to an Unprocessed, GMO-Free Christianity* (Kregel 2016).

He has written dozens of best-selling how-to guides on tech products.

You can connect with him at ScottDouglas.org.

Made in United States
North Haven, CT
04 March 2024

49553793R00076